Joy:
I hope have you have huge success with your business! I hope this

Andy Watson's Moving Guide for Homeowners

An Economical Step-by-Step Plan to Move with Ease!

Andy Watson

For

Laura, Emma, Mom, Dad, Katie and Eric

CONTENTS

ACKNOWLEDGMENTS

I would like to thank everybody that has supported me throughout this wonderful entrepreneurial journey. Just like any entrepreneur will say: it has it's ups and downs but in the end it is always worth it.

My wife, Laura, has been a huge pillar of support through both of the highs and the lows. Some of my biggest struggles came after you and I had met and you're constant support helped me relax and get through the day. During the good days, it was always fantastic to celebrate with you. It still amazes me to this day how easy our relationship can be which allows us to deal with the rest of the world.

Our daughter, Emma, has been an absolute joy as a new addition to our family. Her huge smiles just warm my heart. It is so much fun to hang out with her after a long day.

My parents, Russ and Dori, have been there for me from the beginning. They have provided the encouragement that only parents can provide.

Dad grew up a farmer, and has a great business mind because of it. I remember Dad encouraging me to think about things from the business owner's point of view ever since I started my first job at fourteen years old at Donatos Pizza. Dad is a numbers guy and taught me how to think about profit and loss. Most importantly, he taught me how to work hard for whatever I'm after.

Mom has always been willing to try anything. I have a saying: "What's the worst that could happen?". I relate that to Mom's can-do attitude. Even though it is simply a statement, it has helped me think critically about scenarios to determine the risk. This mindset has given me the confidence to try many things that I probably would have never attempted.

My sister, Katie, and her husband Eric, have always been more than willing to help in any manner they can to support the team effort. Whether it is working a fair booth, mailing letters or simply showing up to help, I can always count on them.

My friends Berg, Billybob, Born, Chris, Tom, and many more throughout the years who have been incredible sounding boards for all the crazy things I have learned.

My different business partners throughout the years have always provided insight and together we have accomplished a lot.

I would finally like to thank the different business coaches I have worked with in the past that helped me progress to where I am today. My current coach, Kevin Hogan, has provided new directions from a unique point of view.

Thank you all!

INTRODUCTION

This book has been put together to help make the moving process smoother. There are some good tips and tricks I have picked up over several moves I have made over the years.

For your ease, I have added a checklist at the end of this book. Please add items to the list that are specific to your needs. There is also a page to write all of your different vendors with the account numbers and phone numbers so you have easy access to everything in one place.

Remember to keep security in mind. When you have any personal information written inside this book, keep it in a safe place. Once you have completed your move, think about shredding the pages with sensitive information.

CHAPTER 1

YOU'RE MOVING!

Congratulations! You have made the decision to move. For many, this is a very exciting time as picking a new place to call home is as personal as it gets. But, now that you have decided on a new place to live, what happens next?

After the excitement of finding a new place wears off, then reality sets in. People start to realize that even though they have only lived in their current place for a few years, they have accumulated A LOT of stuff!

The process of moving can be a daunting task but, with a little planning, it can feel like a well oiled machine needing only minor adjustments along the way.

Moving can be either a short or long process depending on how many personal belongings you own and in how large of a property you reside. Most people have the memories of a parent, grandparent, family friend, or neighbor that have lived in their house for 30, 40 or even 50+ years. Of course, along with these memories comes so many items that it would take days, if not weeks, for a full-time moving crew to remove all of their treasured belongings. For most people, this is a great time to sort through all of your belongings and allow only the truly important items to make it on to the next home. This book will share several ways that will allow you to eliminate unneeded items and even help provide some cash for your move.

Finally, there are several decisions to make that will dictate the manner in how you go about the moving process. It doesn't matter if you are moving because you found your dream house or if you are re-locating for a new job. Most of the items covered in this book will be accomplished either by you or an industry professional on your behalf. You will be able to consider the pros and cons of each option discussed and customize the best moving options for you and your family.

3 Types of Moves

In general, there are three types of moves that most people make. People either move into a new home within the same area, they move away from their current residence but remain within the same state, or they move to a new state. As you would assume, moving to a new place in the same area is the cheapest and easiest move to make. The good news about staying in the same area is you are able to make multiple trips between each property. You can recruit family and friends to help on both sides of the move. You can usually do this without taking any time off from work.

Moving to a new area within 100-150 miles requires more pre-planning and many more logistics that need to happen. You can often accomplish the move easier and cheaper since you can make multiple trips fairly easily. Another advantage of remaining a resident in the same state is that it can make it easier to keep your current hobbies without interruption.

If you are moving to a new state, this can be more of a headache. You will not only have to deal with the stress of moving, but you will have to think about things such as new drivers licenses and professional licensing, among other state regulated activates or licenses. This book will further discuss how to help make this type of move most effectively, especially with the use of the checklist time frame at the end.

3 Ways to Move

Unless you plan to abandon everything that does not fit in your car, then you have a decision to make about how you will make the move. There are three different types of moves. These include moving only with the help of family and friends, hiring a professional company to complete your move for you, or using a hybrid version which includes using both professionals and family and friends.

The first way is to make the move yourself using only family and friends. This may be a great option if you are moving locally since it is easier for friends and family to come and help for short or long periods during a day or weekend. It also can be a huge help if they will be letting you use their vehicles to help transport all of your things. Just make sure to return the favor if they ever request help moving in the future!

The next way is to hire a moving company. Moving companies are by far one of the easiest ways to move. If you are lucky enough to have someone else paying for your move due to a job transfer, moving can be a breeze! However, if you are not in the military or don't have a civilian company flipping the bill, you should be prepared to pay a large amount for this service. With a moving company, you will likely be assigned a "Move Councilor" or "Travel Coordinator". This person will be assigned to your case and do all the scheduling for your move with their company.

Even with a moving company, it will still be important for you to do your research on several companies to make sure one will be the best fit for you. A lot of moving companies are frauds and steal your stuff so check them out through better business bureau and see what their insurance covers if they break your stuff. Start calling early enough before your move so you can get estimates from several companies and find the one that work best with your moving timeframe. Another main thing to consider is if they will be moving your items from your old place directly to your new place? I know of a couple that hired a moving company and then found out all of their belongings were being shipped all across the country for 30 days. They had to live out of a hotel until they finally received their belongings. That was definitely not part of their plan! For these reasons, most of the people I work with tend to move themselves unless their employer is paying for the move.

The final way to move is a hybrid of doing it yourself and hiring a full service moving company. This is the technique I recommend because generally it is the best "bang for your buck" you will find. As long as you or a family member is able to pack most of your things, then this may be the strategy for you. You can do as much as you can such as boxing everything up, driving a rental moving truck and unpacking all of your boxes. You may even be able to borrow a truck and trailer to use if you don't own them yourself. This will be the cheapest but also the most tiring since you are doing all of the packing, loading, driving, unloading, and getting everything settled in your new home.

If you don't want to do the lifting yourself, you can usually find some college or high school students to do the heavy lifting, loading, and unloading of all your boxes and furniture. These students are often looking for some extra cash and student labor is usually cheaper than professional movers. Ask around for some names. Try talking to your family, friends, co-workers, churches or other associations in which you belong. If you can't find people, try posting a Classified Ad in your local newspaper or on Craigslist.

Make sure you check with your insurance company to see if your home owner's policy covers the workers you bring in if one of them should get injured.

During my last move, I had priced out different moving trucks and Penske was the winner. I hired three high school kids to help load everything, but never found the time to find kids in the Washington DC area to help with the unloading process. During my time on the phone with Penske, I heard they offer loading and unloading crews. After I realized we were not going to have the help we needed, I called Penske back. They offered 2 men for a total of 2 hours for only $225. I thought that was a steal! The best part is they are trained professional movers and are insured if they happen to damage any of the items. They also have a small toolbox with them and will assemble (or dismantle) furniture like tables and beds. I couldn't have been more impressed. They were very professional and hard working.

I recommend this third "Hybrid" strategy because moving to a new place is a very demanding task to accomplish. You will be able to oversee the student workers and focus on coordinating the move, which will keep everything running as smoothly as possible. Even though there are a few recommendations about hiring a moving company, this book focuses on the Hybrid Move so I can help give you some ideas on getting the most for your money.

CHAPTER 2

INITIAL PREPARATIONS

Create A Plan

Now that you know where you'll be moving and how you'll be transferring your things, let's create a plan. One of the most common errors I see people make is that they don't adequately prepare for the move, which adds a lot of stress to the move itself. Most people know they'll be moving at least 6-8 weeks prior to the actual date. During this time frame, you should establish a timeline of your move. You can mark a paper calendar or even schedule it in your smartphone calendar program. Do your best to make an educated guess how the process with play out. Just keep in mind that buying and selling houses can have schedule changes along the way for several different reasons.

One of the biggest thing to figure out is how much overlap you will have where you will have possession of both properties at the same time. If there is no overlap, you may want to think about renting a storage unit for that time. A storage unit can be an easy way to store your things without them being in the way. It is also usually much easier to physically move your items in and out of a storage unit than if you would use a friend or family member's house. During a move, you will need as much "easy" in your life as you can. Storage unit rental rates vary widely. Take the time to call around to several storage companies as you may be able to find a much cheaper unit, or even a larger unit for the same price. These companies often have specials depending on their vacancy status. You may even be able to negotiate with them to have the unit for only 1-2 weeks instead of a whole month. Go ahead and schedule a unit so you know it will be ready for you when you need it

CONVENIENCE TIP:

Have your checklist established and start to execute 6-8 weeks prior to your move date. See Addendum A for my checklist to help make your move easier!

Moving Supplies

The next thing you need to think about is boxes. Of course you can buy all the moving boxes you want, but in my opinion that is a waste of money. A lot of people know you can ask your local grocery store to save their boxes for you. However, sometimes these boxes are not the best when used to move with, since you may get boxes such as banana boxes, which have large holes in the top and bottom and don't hold small items very well.

I recommend stopping by any retail store you tend to visit. Furniture stores can be a great source of sturdy boxes. Different restaurants can also have great boxes for moving. You need to make sure you visit them 3-4 weeks before your move to make sure you have enough time. Restaurants in most areas get their deliveries once, sometimes twice a week. In other areas, they may only get their deliveries every 2-3 weeks.

When you talk to these stores, make sure to ask when would be best for you to come pick up the boxes. Most retailers usually break their boxes down and throw them away immediately after they unpack them because they just don't have the room to let them stack up. Restaurants especially don't have extra room. They usually receive their deliveries during the overnight hours and are left on the dining room and walk-in cooler floors. The crew must show up and unpack everything before they are even ready to open, due to the fact they just don't have the extra room. These types of places may be willing to give you the boxes on the condition you have them removed at least 30 minutes before they open for the day. To me, this can be a great trade-off for free boxes!

Of course, along with boxes comes tape. Be sure to buy a good quality packing tape, the extra investment is well worth it to get the higher quality. This is important because the cheapest tape will not stick to the boxes or will come apart during the move. For a few extra dollars, this can save you a lot of headaches! A handheld professional tape dispenser is another item I won't move without. You can get a basic one for $10-$20 and it will speed up your packing time remarkably.

Reservations

The final initial preparation you need to consider is transportation for the move. Do you have access to a truck and trailer that you will be borrowing from friends or family? Do you need to rent a moving truck or trailer? There are a few well-known companies that rent trucks and trailers, and there are a lot of lesser-known companies that can do it, sometimes for a lot cheaper. Do an internet search to see what you can find. Of course, you need to take into account how far you will be moving. Are you moving across town where you can make multiple trips or do you have a 1,500 mile trip to make? Pricing for these trucks and trailers vary, so play around with their online price calculators. Sometimes it is cheaper to pay by the mile than the day and vice versa. Take the extra few minutes to figure out the best bang for your buck. Also, never hesitate to ask for a discount or see if they may be running any specials you didn't find.

No matter which method you decide on, the key is to talk with people in advance and have your plans established. If you'll be using a truck and trailer from friends or family, give them as much notice as you can so they don't make other plans.

Organization

To help keep track of important service information during your move, create a folder or keep a large envelope to hold all of your paperwork and key items. This will keep you organized and help keep stress to a minimum. As part of it, go through all of the services you use such as electric, gas, internet, phone, etc. Next to each service, write down their phone number and your account number on a single page. On a separate page, create a list of all your bills, including credit cards, bank accounts, etc with their phone number and account numbers, but be sure to keep this in a safe place! If you have online access to these accounts, simply create a list of names and services so that you have a list to go down to change your address in the future. This will save you a lot of time so you don't forget one.

If you'll be keeping this information on a computer folder, you'll need to be especially careful. Since computers have come a long way over the recent years, most people are not thinking about backing up their data often, if at all. However, since there is a lot of risk in damaging your computer during a move, you definitely want to back it up one way or another. The big trend recently is to pay for cloud storage. Cloud storage is one of the most convenient forms of backing your data up, especially if you have high speed internet connection. You can also back your data up onto an external hard drive. If you do use an external hard drive, make sure you are extra careful with it during the move. Also, make sure to pack your computer separate from the hard drive in case a freak accident happens and one of the boxes gets destroyed. If you are using a moving company, I would keep your computer and external hard drive with you at all times. Computers are one of the largest security risks we have, so keep that in mind when you are moving them.

Budget

Now that you know what you will need for your move, create a budget. Try to be as detailed as possible when creating your budget. Make sure to include all the estimates you received for the truck and/or trailer, fuel, storage unit, and any additional insurance you may need. If you are using family and friends as "free labor", plan in the expense of all of their meals while they are with you.

Check to see if there will be any tolls you will have to pay during your drive. If you are moving to a new area that has tolls you will be using often, consider buying a transponder that allows you to either use the fast lane at the toll booth or bypass the booth all together. Most of the time, you will save 50% on your tolls by using the transponder. Sometimes that discount is permanent, other times it is only for a set amount of time for new buyers. You can usually buy the transponder online and have it mailed to your current address. It will save you time and money!

After you create an estimate of what the move will cost you, add 10% as a contingency fund. By doing this, it will help the move go as planned without you feeling overwhelmed due to being "Nickel and Dimed to Death" during the middle of the move.

Downsize

Now that you the planning is completed, it's time to start working in the house. Start going through each room individually and decide which items you no longer want or need. There are several disposal methods you can use to get rid of these unwanted items.

One thing I've seen a lot of people forget about is selling all of their unwanted items. You can have a garage or yard sale if the weather permits. If it doesn't, try to find a flea market. You can often find flea markets that are indoors.

If you don't have enough things to sell to make a yard sale or flea market worth your time, take some pictures and place a few ads on Craigslist or on the bulletin boards at your local grocery store, church, etc. You can even advertise that the items are free, but the new owners must move it. This can be a great method for those large or heavy items that you don't want to move yourself. It always amazes me how many people will jump through major hoops just to get something for free.

One of the great things about selling your unwanted items is sometimes people can make enough money to pay for all of their moving expenses.

If you don't want to go through the selling process, you can donate your items to charity. There are several different charities that are always in need of good used items. Some charities even have volunteers that will come pick the items up from your house for free. Donating your stuff to charity not only helps the charity but it will make you feel good in the process.

Finally, there are always items that you have packed away that are damaged, missing pieces, or just not relevant anymore. Those items are best to be thrown away. If you have any items that are too large for your trash man to take away, you may need to take it to your local landfill. If you don't have access to a vehicle that can transport it, just find a suitable place to store it until you are ready to move. Then you can use your moving truck to drop it off at the landfill either on the way or by making a special trip while you're making your main move.

 CONVENIENCE TIP:

Get rid of all your unwanted items by holding a garage sale, selling them online or at a flea market, or donating them to charity.

Take Inventory

After you have gotten rid of everything you won't be taking to your new house, it is time to take inventory. This is a very important step to take in case anything happens to your items because you'll be able to show proof. Make a list of all the contents divided by room. Next, take pictures of those items. To save money, take the pictures of each item on your phone or by using a digital camera. Finally, make sure you back those pictures up either with the cloud or by making copies on your computer.

Review Budget

Since downsizing can take a lot of time, I find it easier to create a budget during the planning process. Now that you don't have as many items, you can make adjustments as needed. Did you get rid of so many things you can make fewer trips? Or maybe you can rent a smaller truck? Once again, be realistic with your expectations. Most people rent a truck that will not haul all their stuff to begin with so don't fall into the trap of downsizing and not being able to move everything!

CHAPTER 3

PREPARING YOUR NEW PLACE

Utilities

Most people do not think about the preparations for their new home early in the process. This is typically a mistake that can delay the move. One of the main things to think about is getting the utilities turned on or switched into your name. You want to make sure you have these essential services running properly without delay. Sometimes they are turned off or are scheduled to be turned off. Depending on the utility company, a lot of times they will send someone to read the meter and switch them into your name without turning them off. This method can save you the "connection fee" which often is at least $50-$75. You should be able to schedule these changes about 4 weeks before.

Ask for a discount. You may qualify for a senior citizen or low income discount. Utility companies have different discounts available so ask while you are setting them up. It may be a pleasant surprise to save a little money every month!

Rehab

A lot of people want to get some basic things accomplished after they take possession of their new place before they start moving in their belongings. Here are a few things to consider.

The first major thing to think about is any kind of rehab you want to do. If this is a major rehab project, you probably won't be moving in at all until after the project is completed. Since these types of projects are typically only performed by investors, odds are you'll only have minor projects you want to complete, such as replacing carpet or painting. This is especially important to consider when and if you are planning to have your things in storage for a period of time so you can make the appropriate reservations. It's important to know the schedule of when these projects will be done so everything can stay on schedule and you'll be in your new home as quickly as possible. You'll want to plan ahead so you can talk to several people (such as for installing carpet) so you can get the right deal and time frame that works best for you.

Cleaning

The most common thing that I have seen people want to do is to clean the property themselves. (Only clean the interior as the exterior can be completed after you move your things in). Keep in mind that it is much easier to clean an empty house compared to one filled with boxes. This is also a great time to clean everything such as the walls, woodwork, windows, light fixture globes, ceiling fan blades, fireplaces, cabinets, and closets inside and out along with your typical cleaning of kitchens and bathrooms.

You may also want to have the carpets professionally steam cleaned. This is also a great time to have the furnace and air conditioner serviced and the system and air ducts cleaned. To save time, you can schedule the furnace and carpet cleaning companies on the same day that you plan to be in the house cleaning the rest of it. Try to have the carpet cleaning scheduled for later in the day so you have a chance to clean all the rooms that have carpet before they show up. You will still have plenty of cleaning to do in the kitchen, bathrooms and other rooms while they are there working.

If you are considering painting one or several rooms, this can be a great time to do it. Once again, it is easier to paint a room before you move your items into it. If you are only looking at one or two rooms you may be able to complete the painting on the same day as you are cleaning, if you have some help. Be sure to allow enough time to clean the room and paint it before the carpet cleaning company shows up. If it is the same day, be sure to tell them the walls have wet paint on them so they don't rub the walls with their hoses.

Door Locks

A common overlooked item is to think about having the exterior door locks changed. If the door handle and locks are of decent quality, you can have a locksmith come out and rekey the same locks. Most purchase agreements specify that a minimum number of keys are passed to the new owners. However, who's to say they don't have an extra spare they forgot about and it gets into the wrong hands. Locksmiths can be a very cheap alternative to having piece of mind for yourself and your family.

Garage Door

Another item I consider to be a security sensitive matter are garage door openers. Just like keys, the remotes are given to the new owners. Most garage door remotes transmit a digital code to the opener head unit. That code is programmed into the opener usually by holding down a button on the opener itself while also holding down the button on the remote. The opener head unit memorized the remote's unique code, then every time it detects the remote being transmitted, it either opens or closes the door.

SAFETY TIP::

Buy all new garage door opener remotes so nobody can use their car remote to open your door!

The problem lies with the new cars that have the garage door remotes installed in the car. To program your car to open your garage door, you must use one of the current remotes to do it. Your car then "memorizes" the special code that your remote transmits, then your car transmits that very same code. Do you see the problem here? You may be given the remote, but their car (or other smart remote) uses that same code to open your garage door! Even though it is not common, they could also program their car from the keypad remote mounted on the outside of the garage.

The only way to remedy this is to clear out the memory on the garage door head unit, then program in brand new remotes (including a new keypad). Do not use the original remotes for this as you would be reprogramming the same code their car currently uses! Depending on the manufacturer, you can usually get new remotes for $20-$40 each.

CHAPTER 4

ESSENTIAL SERVICES

A common thing for people to forget about until it is needed are the essential services you use on a weekly or monthly basis. This is a great time to review all the services you use, close out services if unneeded, and to find services at your new location. You might use this as a reminder to simply find where these services will be located in your new location.

Legal

If you have a local attorney that maintains important documents such a Living Will or Power of Attorney, make sure to get copies of these documents to take with you if you don't already have them. Technology has changed so much, it is easy to keep copies of documents with you at all times. Your attorney may even be able to email a scanned copy of your documents. You can make a special folder within your email account for nothing but those documents. Just make sure someone else, such as a spouse, has a copy of them as well or has a master password so they have access.

Medical

If you are due for an appointment with your doctor, you may want to have that done before you move. Some people use a pending appointment as a way to force them to find a new doctor near their new house. Either way, look into your medical insurance and find out what doctors or hospitals are part of your plan. That way even if you don't need them right away, you will have a Primary Care Physician and other specialists that fit your needs.

Some of the services that are important to look into are pharmacies and oxygen refill services. If you use a chain store for your medications with a branch in your new location, all you need to do is talk to the new or old pharmacist and they can usually transfer your service to the new store for you.

If you use a local pharmacy, be sure to talk to them and let them know you are moving. Even though they are independent, they can help you through the process of transferring your prescriptions to a new company. It is also a good idea to talk to your physician and/or pharmacist to make sure you have enough of each prescription filled so that you won't run out in the first few days of arriving in your new location.

Comfort Items

Schedule your other services to be installed such as security systems, television, and internet services. Although not essential, it's certainly nice to be able to take a break from unpacking and be able to watch your favorite show on television or streamed through the internet.

Pets

Once you have considered all of your important services, it is now time to remember your furry family members. If your pets are due for shots or a check-up, it might be beneficial to get that completed before your move. If so, get a copy of your pet's chart to take to the new Veterinarian. Either way, having your pet records will help to make your move more hassle free when you go to schedule the next vet appointment, nail trimming, daycare, or boarding.

CHAPTER 5

HAVE FUN

Remember, you are leaving a place you have called home for a while now. I'm sure you have had some great memories at your old home. Before you start getting everything torn up and packed away, hold a going away party for your family and friends! This can be a fun way to reminisce before you move to your new place, especially if you are leaving the area!

Even if you have started to pack some items up, you can still hold a little gathering. If the weather is nice, have a barbeque in the back yard. That can keep people out of the different parts of the house that you have started packing. If the weather isn't great, keep the main living areas clean and hold a party there. It doesn't have to be fancy, but a small party with good friends is a great way to help keep your stress levels low!

CHAPTER 6

BOX IT UP

There are probably hundreds if not thousands of techniques and methods used for packing. For the sake of this book I'm going to explain the technique I have used and recommended over the years. The best manner to start packing is early!

If possible, get started by designating a room close to the main exit you will be using and begin to bring all of your packed boxes to this room. For modern houses, this is probably going to be the formal dinning room or formal living room. Typically, these rooms are not used on a daily basis. If you don't have a whole room you can dedicate for a few weeks, find a corner of a room. Use this space to store all of your packed boxes between now and moving day.

If you are using movers you can use QR code stickers and a moving app on your smart phone. This will allow you to list everything in each box. The great part of using the QR codes is that it makes every box look the same. This is important so that other people will have no idea what is in each box and they won't be tempted to steal it. If you are moving all your own things, then using a black marker will work just fine.

Start packing early (up to 8 weeks out). There are numerous items you have in your house that you do not use on an ongoing basis. Items you can start to pack up are decorations, holiday items, spare bedroom supplies, DVDs and even pictures you have hung on the walls.

Essential Items

Avoid packing up any cleaning supplies you will need for the first day in your new place. Don't forget to also include a ladder and a flashlight with these items. You will want to make sure these items are set aside so they are not buried in a moving truck. You can even have a different room as the "critical item" section. Include a vacuum, cleaning chemicals, paper towels, trash bags, sponges and a toilet brush.

It's also important to set aside essential non-cleaning items. These may include toilet paper, towels, hand soap, and paper plates for eating or snacks while you're getting the cleaning finished. Even though all of your belongings won't be unpacked, having these essential items can still help make it feel like home!

CONVENIENCE TIP:

Place the QR Code or Write the Box Contents on the side of the boxes so you can see them while stacked up.

As time gets closer, pack your suitcases with all of the essential clothes you will need to live through the first 3 days in your new house. This will allow you to focus on the move instead of wasting valuable time searching for clean clothes.

CHAPTER 7

WRAPPING UP YOUR OLD PLACE

Once your things are all moved out, you will want to place any user guides and instruction manuals that will be staying in your old house somewhere that will be easily found by the new owners. These may include warranty information for appliances, the hot water tank, furnace, and anything else that stays with the property.

Make sure to check your mail one last time too although hopefully you have already forwarded your mail to the new address by this point.

Cleaning

Once everything is moved out, you will want to do a quick cleanup for the new owners. Make sure to clean anything you see that needs it including walls, windows, switches, mirrors, toilets, showers, and sinks. Also mop the floors and vacuum the carpet. There are a lot of people that don't do any cleaning at all. To me, this is a respect issue for the new owners. They bought your house at a fair price (hopefully), so take the time so they get their new dream home in tip-top shape.

CHAPTER 8

UPDATE CONTACT INFO

Once you are sure the closing will happen (sometimes they do fall through for different reasons, even on the day of closing), then it is time to change your contact information. The first one you may want to change is your driver's license. Sometimes you can register to vote at the same time. Use the checklist you created at the beginning of your moving process to change your address either over the phone or online. Don't forget to change your contact information with banks, insurance companies, magazine subscriptions, etc.

Apply for any new licenses that you may need, including things such as dog tags.

The other items you may want to think about changing are your online accounts such as Amazon, Facebook and LinkedIn. Once you make the address change with your bank, anything you have on a recurring payment plan with a credit card will probably be declined unless you update your billing address with each vendor. It may be easiest to scroll through your bank statement to identify everyone that receives payments. If it is a service you no longer need or use, just go ahead and cancel that service and save yourself the money.

If you decide to change your cell phone number, this would be a good time to do it. You will save a lot of time updating your contact information if you can do both your address and phone number at the same time.

Don't forget about your friends and family as well. A fun way to send notification that you have moved is to take a picture of yourselves in front of your new house. You can send that out in an email or text, updating your address and phone number all at the same time.

CHAPTER 9

FINALLY IN!

Recycle

Once you finish unpacking things into your new house, don't forget all of those moving boxes. You can recycle them in several ways. If they are in good condition and could be used to help somebody else move, list them for free on Craigslist. If they are not in good condition, you can take them to your local recycling center.

Party Time

You have completed your move so now it is time to relax! If you moved locally, hold a house warming party for all of your family and friends.

If you have moved to a new city it is time to start meeting some new friends. There are several ways you can meet new people today compared to what was available even 15 years ago.

First, ask yourself what activities you truly enjoy. The nice thing is that there are groups for about every activity out there and a lot of them advertise themselves on MeetUp.com. Another great way to meet local people is during your children's activities. Have them get involved in school activities and maybe hang out for the practices to get to know the other parents.

Another great way to meet people is through local events. Most communities hold events that you can attend for free. You can usually get the brochures and guides from the visitor's bureau and/or Chamber of Commerce.

There are also computer apps that are geared for small communities such as a subdivision. Find out if your community is part of one and if not, maybe start one up. They are great to get the word out about different things such as events, lost pets, or advice on door-to-door salesmen.

One idea I had is to hold a Meet and Greet in your front yard on a Saturday afternoon. Hang a poster board on your mailbox advertising free hot dogs and lemonade. People love free stuff so that is one way for sure you would get a good turnout and have a lot of fun in the process!

Before you know it, you will feel like a local within your new community. Just try to be open minded at first as you don't know who you might meet!

APPENDIX A

MOVING CHECKLIST

Moving Checklist

Initial Planning

Make Timeline	☐
Schedule Family & Friends	☐
Schedule Truck/Trailer	☐
Schedule Storage Unit	☐
Schedule Movers	☐
Buy Supplies (Tape, Markers, QR Stickers)	☐
Get Free Boxes	☐
Sell/Donate Your Unwanted Stuff	☐
Create Inventory with Pictures	☐
Schedule Babysitting	☐
Schedule Pet Boarding	☐

A Few Weeks Before

Transfer Services	☐
Notify Proper Businesses of Change of Address	☐
Cancel Local Newspaper	☐
Get Moving Boxes	☐

3 Days Before

Call and Confirm all Reservations
(Including Friends)
Do All Laundry
Pack Suitcase with Essential Clothes & Toiletries
Finish Packing Everything Else
Clean Old House
Forward Mail
Return Rented Equipment (DVRs, etc.)
Schedule Locksmith for New House

Day Before

Do Final Laundry
Pack Up Remaining Items other than Suitcase

Moving Day

Pack up all toiletries and clothes
Take Kids & Pets to Babysitting/Boarding
Pick up items (moving truck/trailer)

Settling In

Change Locks
Clear Garage Door Opener Memory &
Program New Remotes (including Keypad)
Change Driver's License
Register to Vote

Change Address for:

Bank Account(s)	
Insurance Policies	
Retirement Account(s)	
Credit Cards	
Personal Loans	
Car Loans	
Trade Groups	
Magazine/Catalog Subscriptions	
Online Accounts (Amazon, LinkedIn, etc.)	
Veteran's Administration	
Attorney(s)	
Medical Professionals	
Veterinarian(s)	
Religious Group(s)	
Employer(s)	
Schools/Colleges/Universities	
Alumni Associations	
Charities/Non-Profits	

BIBLIOGRAPHY

Hogan, Kevin. *The Secret Language of Business,* Hoboken: John Wiley & Sons, Inc., 2008. Print.

Lechter, Sharon L. and Greg S. Reid. *Three Feet from Gold,* New York: Sterling, 2009. Print.

Hill, Napoleon. *Outwitting the Devil*, New York: Sterling, 2011. Print

Shankwitz, Frank. *Wishman,* Las Vegas: Sherpa Press, 2016. Print

Klein, Arlene. *The Grandfather of Possibilities,* Sarasota: Arlene Klein, 2014.

Corbin, David M. *Illuminate,* Hoboken: John Wiley & Sons, Inc., 2009. Print.

INDEX

M

Making a Special Trip, 13

Medical, 19, 35

Minor Projects, 16

Move Councilor, 3

Moving App, 25

Moving Checklist, 33

Moving Company, 3-5, 11

Moving Day, 25, 34

Moving Process, 2, 29

Moving Supplies, 8

Moving to a New Place, 2, 5

Moving to a New State, 2

N

New Drivers Licenses, 2

New Home, 2, 4, 15-16

New State, 2

P

Q-R

U

V-Z

Old House - Utility Companies Numbers

Electric   Phone No. _____

                      Account _____

Gas   Phone No. _____

                      Account _____

TV Service   Phone No. _____

                      Account _____

Internet Service   Phone No. _____

                      Account _____

Security System   Phone No. _____

                      Account _____

Phone   Phone No. _____

                      Account _____

Garbage   Phone No._____

                 Account _____

Other   Phone No._____

                 Account _____

Other   Phone No._____

                 Account _____

Other   Phone No._____

                 Account _____

Other   Phone No._____

                 Account _____

Other   Phone No._____

                 Account _____

AndyWatsonOnline.com

New House - Utility Companies Phone Numbers

Electric   Phone No. _____

Account _____

Gas   Phone No. _____

Account _____

TV Service   Phone No. _____

Account _____

Internet Service   Phone No. _____

Account _____

Security System   Phone No. _____

Account _____

Phone   Phone No. _____

Account _____

Garbage   Phone No. _____

                 Account _____

Other   Phone No. _____

                 Account _____

Other   Phone No. _____

                 Account _____

Other   Phone No. _____

                 Account _____

Other   Phone No. _____

                 Account _____

Other   Phone No. _____

                 Account _____

NOTES

NOTES

_____

_____

_____

_____

_____

_____

_____

_____

_____

_____

_____

_____

_____

_____

_____

_____

_____

NOTES

_____

_____

_____

_____

_____

_____

_____

_____

_____

_____

_____

_____

_____

_____

_____

_____

_____

NOTES

NOTES

NOTES

_____

_____

_____

_____

_____

_____

_____

_____

_____

_____

_____

_____

_____

_____

_____

_____

ABOUT THE AUTHOR

Andy Watson has been investing in real estate ever since his parents, Russ and Dori Watson, bought their first rental house in 1999. Together, they have been doing all different types of real estate investments all across the United States. They have had rental houses, buy/fix/sell (flips), lease/options, and non-performing notes/ mortgages (buying the bad loans from the banks).

After graduating from the University of North Dakota with a degree in Aviation, Andy became an Air Traffic Controller at Cleveland ARTCC (Center) for seven years. During that time, Andy worked alongside his parents in real estate.

Today, Andy has moved to Northern Virginia near Washington D.C. and is excited to start raising his family there. Andy continues to invest in real estate and is a Keynote Speaker.

To contact Andy or find out more information to have Andy as your next speaker, go to www.AndyWatsonOnline.com.